THOUGHTS FROM AN EMPTY HEAD

DON'T BE A DUMMY!

THE UNBELIEVABLE LIFE OF BASKET EDDY

as told to CLIFFORD IRVING

Beverly • Seattle • Bellagio

[product]

a [product] book

ISBN 979-8-9888674-3-2 trade paperback
ISBN 979-8-9888674-2-5 hardcover edition

Printed via the mighty and majestic Ingram Spark
10 9 8 7 6 5 4 3 2 1 Czech

Basket Eddy photographed by Arkadi Bojaršinov / Dreamstime.com

Don't Be A Dummy is a work of extreme fiction. Names, characters, businesses, places, events, locales, and incidents are either the products of the author's imagination or used in a fictitious manner. Any resemblance to actual persons, living or dead, or actual events is purely coincidental. I.e., Basket Eddy never met Clifford Irving.

ARE YOU READY FOR BASKET EDDY? AGAIN?

Ever since an enigmatic group of high school juniors put up a mannequin named Basket Eddy for junior class president of New Canaan High School in 1973 — and won — the world has been asking, "Whatever happened to Basket Eddy?" (Well, a few people, anyway.)

A few months after the election, a hand-addressed letter was received — intercepted? — by the vertically challenged Vice Principal of NCHS. This was after Basket Eddy became known to a larger swath of the general public due to a few newspaper articles appearing as "interviews" with Mr. Eddy. Interviews full of all the wit and wisdom one could possibly wring from the situation and the participants. Notably, the archives show, the "interviews" are dotted with a few brilliant sparkles amidst the usual lame inside jokes and "borrowed" passages from National Lampoon articles and Monty Python scripts one was apt to hear from High School students in the 1970s.

It should be noted, Mr. NCHS Vice Principal was dead-set against the Class Presidency of yet another dummy, this one an air-head "for reals," as they said back then. And Eddy was a hand taller, which irked him no end. Which was why, when Eddy and his acolytes opened the note, and the name Clifford Irving appeared to be scrawled at the bottom, they considered the letter a forgery claiming to be from the author of — you can't make this shit up — *The Autobiography of Howard Hughes*, one of the more famously bogus books.

But, no. Irving did indeed want to nab the rights to Eddy's life and likeness.

After some tense telephone calls by Irving's representatives with the sentient beings in the room, who it should be noted were lubricated by liquid refreshments bought with impressive, though fake, I.D.s and passed around joints of now legal, though not back then in the 1970s, uncontrolled substances, the deal was done. Dollars wired. Deposited. Spent. Basket Eddy jetted off, first class, in fact, to a secret location off the southern coast of Spain.

Years later, Irving claimed the manuscript was lost in a boating accident, or was it a house fire, or was it a boat accident-cum-explosion causing a house fire: those on the call reported no one could hear very well due to the static, cross-talk, and flanging happening with the awful transatlantic connection. (Or, more likely, it was the spliffs talking.)

But what is this? After almost half a century and under a moldering couch cushion in a Paris garret, the pages were found. Basket Eddy's biography; the book with all the details writ large with as much breathless prose able to be crammed into one manuscript before the Pesetas ran out: the drugs, the sex, spying for the C.I.A., making feature films for Kim Il-Sung, a stint as a turnpike toll-collector/drug dealer, the millions made and spent; a fantastically lush life.

At last, the tale of Basket Eddy's genuinely unbelievable life, as told to *that* Clifford Irving, which the world has been waiting to read. (Well, a few people, anyway.)

"Why not?"

BASKET EDDY

CLIFFORD MICHAEL IRVING, born on November 5, 1930, was a native New Yorker whose love for writing blossomed early in life. After graduating from Cornell University in 1951 with a degree in American Literature, Irving embarked on a remarkable literary journey. Some might attribute this odyssey to his quest for an escape from the mundane rhythms of conventional work. In contrast, others would credit his extraordinary talent for weaving fiction into reality, often in the company of captivating women as he traveled around the world.

Leaving Cornell, he began his career as a copyboy at the New York Times but soon set out on an unconventional path, choosing a more affordable and sexier life. Ibiza afforded. It was on this Mediterranean island that Irving penned his debut novel, *On a Darkling Plain* (1956).

Irving is best known for his audacious attempt to craft a fabricated autobiography of the elusive billionaire Howard Hughes, an adventure he later called "a writing odyssey." Claiming to have conducted exclusive and intimate interviews with Hughes, Irving secured a publishing deal with McGraw-Hill. After Hughes emerged from seclusion to vehemently disown the book, Irving's extravagant deception was exposed, leading to his arrest. The incriminating testimony given by his then-lover, the singer and actress Nina Van Pallandt, at the trial, sealed his fate as well as his divorce from his then-wife Edith Sommer.

Following his 17-month incarceration, Irving rekindled his writing career, producing a diverse array of novels and non-fiction works. Resilient and determined not to be defined solely by his lies and deceptions, he, along with his partner in crime Richard Suskind, swiftly authored *Project Octavio* (1977), recounting the true events surrounding the fabricated Hughes autobiography. During this period, he crossed paths with the enigmatic figure known as Basket Eddy, who was then hiding out in a splendid suburb of Connecticut. Through a promising advance against royalties, Eddy became his ward.

Clifford Irving's life came to an end on December 19, 2017, in Sarasota, Florida, USA, due to complications from pancreatic cancer. Julie Irving (Schnall), his surviving widow, uncovered the existence of the Paris garret within his archives, leading to the discovery of this manuscript and a treasure trove of interviews between Clifford, Eddy, and Irving's various lovers of the late 1970s and early 1980s.

Despite, or because of, the scandal and notoriety surrounding the Hughes hoax, Irving continues to captivate those intrigued by literary deceptions and controversies, as well as his body of published works, which as you may have guessed, does not includes the blank book you are holding.

Books by CLIFFORD IRVING

On a Darkling Plain (1956)
(also published in Canada as The Quick and the Loving)

The Losers (1958)

The Valley (1960)

The 38th Floor (1965)

The Battle of Jerusalem (1967)

Spy (1968)

Fake (1969)
The Story of Elmyr de Hory:
The Greatest Art Forger of Our Time

Autobiography of Howard Hughes (1971)

Project Octavio (1972)
The Story of the Howard Hughes Hoax
with Richard Suskind

The Death Freak (1976)

The Sleeping Spy (1979)

The Hoax (1981)

Tom Mix and Pancho Villa (1981)

The Angel of Zin (1983)

Trial (1987)

Daddy's Girl (1988)
The Campbell Murder Case. A True Tale of Vengeance,
Betrayal, and Texas Justice

Final Argument (1990)

The Spring (1995)

Boy on Trial (2004)

Clifford Irving's Prison Journal, aka Jailing (2012)

Bloomberg Discovers America (2012)

Don't Be A Dummy (2023)
The Unbelievable Life of Basket Eddy
As Told to Clifford Irving
(A blank book you should be doodling in by now.)

www.ingramcontent.com/pod-product-compliance
Lightning Source LLC
Chambersburg PA
CBHW060857120626
46553CB00001B/112
9798988867432